D1339379

THE BRIDAL SUITE

THE BRIDAL SUITE

Matthew Sweeney

CAPE POETRY

First published 1997

1 3 5 7 9 10 8 6 4 2

© Matthew Sweeney 1997

Matthew Sweeney has asserted his right
under the Copyright, Designs and Patents Act 1988
to be identified as the author of this work

First published in the United Kingdom in 1997 by
Jonathan Cape,
Random House, 20 Vauxhall Bridge Road, London SW1V 2SA

Random House Australia (Pty) Limited
20 Alfred Street, Milsons Point, Sydney,
New South Wales 2061, Australia

Random House New Zealand Limited
18 Poland Road, Glenfield,
Auckland 10, New Zealand

Random House South Africa (Pty) Limited
Endulini, 5A Jubilee Road, Parktown 2193, South Africa

Random House UK Limited Reg. No. 954009

A CIP catalogue record for this book
is available from the British Library

Papers used by Random House UK Limited are natural,
recyclable products made from wood grown in sustainable forests.
The manufacturing processes conform to the environmental
regulations of the country of origin.

ISBN 0 224 04328 5

Typeset by Palimpsest Book Production Limited,
Polmont, Stirlingshire
Printed and bound in Great Britain by
Creative Print and Design (Wales), Ebbw Vale

FOR ROSEMARY

Oh, Oh, Oh! she cried . . .
Is this what you call
making me comfortable?

William Carlos Williams

CONTENTS

The Bells   1
The Sea   2
Reconfirming Light   3
Never in Life   4
The Bridal Suite   5
The Glass Coffin   6
The Long-Legged Chair   7
Sleep with a Suitcase   8
In a Field   9
Try Biting   10
Riding into Town   11
Princess   12
The Box   13
Upstairs   14
The House   15
Grandpa's Bed   16
Poker   17
Writing to a Dead Man   18
The Hat   20
Bagpipes   21
Meat   22
The Wobble   23
Chinese Opera   24
A Blur   25
Our Ikky   26
The Mules   27
Initiation   28
Reading   29
Donkey Hoof   30

The Blue Taps	31
Friday Bed	32
The Compromise	33
Goodbye to the Sky	34
Dancer	36
Pincushion	37
Russian	38
The Dog	39
Crossing	40
Postcards	41
An End	42
Elm	43
The Butcher	44
A Picnic on Ice	45
Skylight	46
Skating	47
Keep Him In	48
The Bat	49

ACKNOWLEDGEMENTS

Acknowledgements are due to the editors of the following:

Cyphers, The Devil, Grand Street, Harvard Review, Honest Ulsterman, Independent, London Magazine, London Review of Books, New Orleans Review, New Statesman, New Writing 5 (Vintage), *New Yorker, Pivot, Poetry, Poetry Ireland Review, Poetry Review, Poetry Wales, Southern Review, Sunday Times, Upstart, Yale Review*

Three of the poems, 'The Blue Taps', 'In a Field' and 'Writing to a Dead Man', were published separately, as a limited edition – *The Blue Taps* – by Clarion Publishing, with illustrations by John Ross.

'Skating' was commissioned by the Poetry Society for 'publication' on the Internet. Several of the poems were read on various BBC Radio 3 or 4 programmes, and one was commissioned by the World Service.

THE BELLS

for John Hartley Williams

Fighting the undertow,
watching the boat drift away,
the monk felt his habit grow
heavy as a suit of armour,
and struggled till he was naked,
hoping his fat would keep him
alive in the ice-berged Atlantic
until he caught the toe of rock
that kicked the sea to Ireland.
He clung to a plastic lunchbox
and thought of the veal pies
famous in the monastery, hoping
his surfeit years were enough
to keep him awake for five hours.
He thought of his antics
with the boy, behind the shed
where his boat was kept
waiting for today. He felt
his fingers get pins and needles
and his testicles go numb,
his feet become bare bone
and his eyes start to close.
He was so tired now,
already he heard the bells ring
in the distant fog. If he slept
he'd float there, in time for mass.

THE SEA

Sitting on an upturned boat
in the green middle of a roundabout
overlooked by towers and crenellations,
she watched the cars curve by
and waited. Overhead, the gulls
kaokaoed the blue of the sky
where fat clouds floated, and a lone bee
was higher than ever before.
She looked at her handbag watch
just as a truckdriver hooted.
She glanced towards Aberdeen.
She felt the keys in her bag
and thought of the house on the island
where six years ago she'd eaten
an omelette of twelve quails' eggs
washed down with Chablis.
She'd hardly get there tonight.
Old pictures assaulted her,
floated in the haze – memories of
twenty or more black sheep
in a field that stopped at the sea.
. And hundreds of gulls spread out
behind a ploughing tractor.
And a herd of lying-down cows.
And a cemetery in a golf course
that bordered the sea. All these
were waiting, but she was stuck
in the green middle of the roundabout,
sitting on the upturned boat,
and the sea stayed where it was.

RECONFIRMING LIGHT

for Tom Lynch

On Mullett Lake in mid-March
two pickups are parked by blue ice-shanties.
Fishermen are inside. Perch
and walleye are what they're after
through their holes in the ice, although
a week, two weeks from now is best,
right before the ice melts and thermal
inversion sends the fish wild.
And shanties and pickups go under.

Down there, deep, cruise the sturgeon,
big as torpedos. They're never seen
except when they lounge on the top
to reconfirm light, or when a hook
snags one and a boat's tugged in circles.
Slowly though. There are worse catches –
corpses that lie on the bottom all winter
then float up to be towed in,
wearing clothes a size too small for them.

NEVER IN LIFE

For eight days the sea held him,
or what was left of him,
for eight days the sea moved him about
through miles of underwater,
far from land, then close again,
till it left him afloat on his back
at the base of a cliff.

Before that, seals had circled
above where he'd settled,
alerting a Christian Brother diver
who hadn't gone deep enough
into the submerged wrack.

Two more had been with him
in the storm-tossed boat,
but they were waked already,
were stuck in blessed ground.
He had been given up
until the sheep boy saw him.

Never in life had he drawn a crowd
like the one spread out
along the clifftop, to witness
a door being dropped on ropes
then raised again with him tied on,
before being carried by six men
at the head of a procession,
a mile uphill to an ex-dancehall
which was ours.

THE BRIDAL SUITE

For Nuala Ní Dhomnaill

On the third night in the bridal suite
without the bride, he panicked.
He couldn't handle another dream like that,
not wet, like he'd expected,
but not dry either – men digging holes
that they'd fill with water, donkeys
crossing valleys that suddenly flooded.
The alarm-call had a job to wake him,
to send him out from the huge bed,
past the corner kissing-sofa, up two steps
to the shower he hardly needed,
where he'd scrub himself clean as the baby
he'd hoped to start that night,
under the canopy like a wimple,
in that room of pinks and greens.
Naked and dripping, he'd rung Reception
to see if she'd rung, then he'd stood
looking out at the new marina,
as if he'd glimpse her on a yacht.
On the third night he could take no more –
he dressed, to the smell of her perfume,
and leaving her clothes there,
the wedding dress in a pile in the wardrobe,
he walked past the deaf night porter,
out to his car. He had no idea
where he was headed, only that she,
if she ever came back, could sample
the bridal suite on her own,
could toss in that canopied bed
and tell him about her dreams.

THE GLASS COFFIN

The Brocagh boys
are carrying one of their number
in a glass coffin.
They are taking him
to his caravan, the best place
to wake him in.
They can see him
lying on his left side
facing the mountain.
One is pushing
his antiquated bicycle
behind the coffin.
They will go in the grave together,
first the bicycle,
then the glass coffin.
His third nervous breakdown
was his last one.
He won't ask again
how to spell three.
He won't fall in a sheugh
when he's in the grave.
The Brocagh girls
are leaving the factory
to wake him.
They are shouting
about nylons, for the legs,
for the thighs.
Some have bottles,
some have tyres
for a funeral blaze.
They follow the glass coffin
and the boys
up the steps of the caravan.

THE LONG-LEGGED CHAIR

She bought a long-legged chair
and painted it red. And no one
but her could sit there,
head at the highest pane,
above the pictures of Marilyn,
above the mirror. She ate there,
fed herself boiled eggs,
babytalking all the while.
Sometimes she'd rock so hard
she'd almost fall. She liked
to listen to Mozart up there,
holding her head in her hands.
She went out less and less
and had no one round. Friends
gave up calling the ansaphone
that she heard from the chair,
then nothing, not a ring.
Once the doorbell went
but she was asleep up there,
woke to stare at the door,
seeing the cup-hook
and the judo-belt hanging
at just the height of the chair.

SLEEP WITH A SUITCASE

I slept with a suitcase last night.
It didn't snore. It was half-packed
and there was a map on the floor.
Outside, snow covered the roof
of my tanked-up car. I kept
my clothes on and the heating up,
and the phone off the hook.
I wanted no one and nothing
between me and the morning.
I set my alarm for the dawn.
The poison I fed the cat
was working in the dark kitchen.
The mailbox was in the trash.
I left a note on the oven
saying I was dead, forgotten,
and the house was my son's.
He would sleep for three days
then wake with a headache.
I left him aspirin and water,
and his father's phone number,
or the last one I knew.

IN A FIELD

A shoelace and a penis lying in a field
on a cold, blue, February morning.
Is it hours, or days the police will take to find them?
And the shoes, the other lace, the rest of the man –
where are they in the crisp sunshine
(Conrad's favourite weather) while seagulls
cruise at sixty feet, at the furthest they've been inland
and a mouse, with eyes on the sky, sniffs the penis,
scurries away, along tyre-tracks,
through stubble, weaving, darting.
Which of the five murders, all with missing bodies,
that compete with Maastricht for the headlines,
is this fine one? Does anyone
know yet the penis is gone?
When the farmer, taking a shortcut home,
comes across it will he know what it is?
Will he pick it up in a hanky
and accelerate to the police?
And they, will they have a clue who it belongs to?
After poking at it, and peering at it, and scratching
and laughing, will they freeze it
till later, till they find bodies to check,
till a widow comes shaking and sobbing
and the penis and the rest of the body
go into the ground, or into fire together,
and slowly become forgotten?

TRY BITING

'Try biting,' said the sailor
to the man he'd tied up,
after punching out his teeth,
and pocketing his wallet,
and pulling on his jeans.
'Where's your passport, shit?
You've left it at home!'
So he kicked him again,
and when the man cried out
he kicked him again.
Then he gagged him
with the bloodstained shirt,
and when a dog came nosing
it got kicked, too,
and scurried, yelping,
out of the alleyway.
And the sailor laughed,
then tightened his belt,
before spitting on the man
and heading into town.
He'd have a few good ones,
he thought, beers first,
then whisky. And a woman.
He stopped beneath a streetlight
to admire his jeans,
then turned to a window
to tidy his hair, and grin –
a wide, ivoried grin.

RIDING INTO TOWN

The whistle of the bottle through the air,
the double-smash of glass, the screaming –
all this went through him like a breath,
in and out of his switched-off ears.
He was riding his horse through the town,
he didn't care what went on there –
the drunks taking chairs to each other,
the women in leggings, the policemen.

He had come here to smash the arms
of the statue that guarded the graveyard –
the statue of Our Lady of Prague
that had stood here since he was a kid.
With the noise, no one would hear him,
and no one came here after dark.
He peered skywards, and fondled the head
of the sledge concealed in his greatcoat.

PRINCESS

The boy who lives in the wrecked bus
down on the rocks, near the point
knows every yard of the long beach
that curves to the ruined castle
where the girl's skeleton lies
behind a wall – a false wall
that only the boy's discovered,
and only he knows the loose stones
that lift out to let him in,
so he can comb the long red hair
that's still attached to the skull,
and he brings her what he's found
that day on the beach, and calls her
what she was, Princess, even when
they walled her up in her room
and left her to die, alone
until the boy found her, and now
she's visited every day, and lies
surrounded by buoys, lifejackets,
lobster-floats, two odd shoes
(one with a bony foot still in it),
half of an oar, a rubber dingy
and a driftwood sculpture the boy made
on the day he guessed was her birthday
because of the rainbow he saw
ending at the castle, as he left the bus
and ran the three miles to her,
and the rainbow went as he got there.

THE BOX

79 years in a cast-iron box
in the basement of an old hotel
that was once the best in Donegal –
and only the porter could open the lock
to reveal what was in the box
and you wouldn't have guessed for a gillion
that a broken-up skeleton was in there
holding its skull in its hands,
with its legs folded beneath it,
and in the box alongside it
a yellowy scroll of pig's leather
sound as the day it was tanned.

It fell to the hotel manager
to read the scroll. A throat-clearing,
then a voice: *Here sits folded*
Magnus McLaughlin, who did
more skitterish deeds in his life
than an English blackguard,
and so I built this box myself
to keep him in, and I chopped him
with the cleaver I kept for pork
and you should have seen the blood.
She paused, and added *March 1913.*
And we all stared at the box.

UPSTAIRS

Last year I was going downstairs,
now I'm going upstairs. Up there
is a rocking horse in red velvet.
I'll dust him off with a crow's wing,
then I'll shake the kitchen ceiling.
I'll jump off in mid-buck, onto
the round water-bed I bounced on
with black-haired, patchouli-scented X
to the drawl of Mick Jagger.
I'll take the brass telescope to the window
to see if Mrs Voss is still undressing
with the blind drawn to her neck.
I'll fit together the owl-kite
and, opening the window, I'll feed
the kite to the sea wind,
wondering if it'll reach Iceland.
I'll rummage under the newspapers
till I find the carpenter's set
my Grandpa bought me, the saw
just right for severing flex.
I'll take a swig from the hip-flask,
then, locking the door, I'll switch
the light on, and I'll start sawing
three inches above the bulb.

THE HOUSE

The house had a dozen bedrooms,
each of them cold, and the wind
battered the windows and blew down
power-lines to leave the house dark.
Rats lived in the foundations,
sending scouts under the stairs
for a year or two, and once
a friendly ghost was glimpsed
at the foot of a bed. Downhill
half a mile was the Atlantic,
with its ration of the drowned –
one of whom visited the house,
carried there on a door.
It hosted dry corpses, too,
with nostrils huge to a child,
but never a murder –
except the lambs bled dry
in the yard outside. Sunlight
never took over the interior,
and after dark the cockroaches
came from under a cupboard
to be eaten by the dog.
Crows were always sitting
on the wires, planning nests
in the chimneys, and a shotgun
sometimes blew a few away.
Neighbours never entered
as often as in other houses,
but it did have a piano upstairs.
And I did grow up there.

GRANDPA'S BED

My granny was my ally.
She'd help me out the window
and leave it open.
She didn't mind how long
I stayed, or what I did.
I could have slept with you
in her bed. Instead
I'd jump to the ground
and make for the graveyard,
lit by its one streetlight
on the edge of town.
It would be locked, of course,
but a pig had bent two bars
trying to get in. I'd creep
round the back of the church,
then, in the dark, I'd count
tombstones until my fingers
spelt out Grandpa's name.
While I waited, I told him
everything about you,
and asked his permission
to do what we did above him.
Then you'd arrive, shivering
even though it was summer,
whispering this was madness,
till we went down on Grandpa's bed.

POKER

There were five of us playing that night,
Padge, Kieran, Neal and me –
and, stretched out in his coffin, Uncle Charlie.
We dealt him a hand each time
and took it in turns to bet for him,
waiving his losses, pooling his wins,
for what good were coins to him?
What could he win but his life?
Still, five of us played that night
and when we stopped it was daylight.
We left the cards with him
to remind him, forever, of that game
and Padge, Kieran, Neal and me
went up the road to our beds
and slept until we buried him,
then played until we had to agree
the good hands had gone with Uncle Charlie.

WRITING TO A DEAD MAN

i.m. Raymond Tyner

I want to write to a dead man.
I want to recommend a book,
and slip in a potted 5-year history
of the world since him. I see him,
when I close my eyes, in a hammock –
that old Rastafarian hammock –
on our roof garden. He's naked
and reading Schopenhauer, with a cold
beer on the floor. He hears
an aircraft noise, then a voice
through a megaphone – a police voice,
telling him to get some clothes on.
He wrote me this in dudgeon
and did I answer? I want to
tell him I've sat in a car outside
the house he lived in, and eaten
in his favourite Chinese restaurant,
and heard the ignominious stories
of his last weeks – sleep in the office,
no home, linen hanging to dry
in full view of students. I recall
telephone conversations of that time,
his plans that could have included
burial on the moon, his riches
banked in his head. I reckon now
he'll be over that. Five years
in the earth of Georgia would cure that.
I'm sure of it. I want to tell him
I don't hold his last months against him,
and I think of him when I eat salmon,
and I now agree with him about Swift,

and he was wrong about Ireland,
about my coldness there, after we'd
visited Lisadell, and the Tower,
and stood at Yeats' grave. I want
to argue with him, gently,
and the best way is in a letter.
I know he saw ghosts in our flat
but I don't want to see him.
I don't mind that he won't write back.

THE HAT

A green hat is blowing through Harvard Square
and no one is trying to catch it.
Whoever has lost it has given up –
perhaps, because his wife was cheating,
he took it off and threw it like a frisbee,
trying to decapitate a statue
of a woman in her middle years
who doesn't look anything like his wife.
This wind wouldn't lift the hat alone,
and any man would be glad to keep it.
I can imagine – as it tumbles along,
gusting past cars, people, lampposts –
it sitting above a dark green suit.
The face between them would be bearded
and not unhealthy, yet. The eyes
would be green, too – an all green man
thinking of his wife in another bed,
these thoughts all through the green hat,
like garlic in the pores, and no one,
no one pouncing on the hat to put it on.

BAGPIPES

The bagpipes on the wall began to skirl
the minute she reversed out the drive.
She took with her nothing but her spaniel
and the walnut clock, but they were enough
to convince him she was gone for good.
He stood watching as she swerved away,
out towards the sheep-encrusted headland
where she'd sat every day and painted
portraits of the waves, but today he knew
she wouldn't stop there, was only going
to skid a goodbye, before booting it south
to somewhere he wouldn't be. The bagpipes
droned on, needing no mouth to rouse them.
There was more than one set, clearly –
he'd gatecrashed a bagpipers' convention
in his own home, that was no home now.
He started to scream his accompaniment.
He threw a few mugs at the wall
and took the poker to the mirror.
Beneath it, the voodoo mask was laughing
like he always knew it would. She'd bought it.
She would never take that with her.
He looked at it, and ran at the window.
The bagpipes drowned out the breaking glass.

MEAT

I sent a pig's head to my mother-in-law.
A week later I sent two cows' eyes in a box.
I gave her no clue of my identity,
and didn't tell my wife. She heard soon enough –
a crying on the phone halfway through dinner,
and I choked on a boar sausage, laughing,
while my wife turned round and glared.

It was like good mustard when she told me.
As she spoke I knew what I'd send next –
lambs' testicles. One by one I'd send her mother
all my grandfather's favourites: snipe, rabbit,
ox tail, chitterlings and blood from a pig.
I hoped she hadn't thrown out her recipes.
How did she think she could renounce meat?

THE WOBBLE

Halfway across the ravine,
watched by more than a thousand
and a further million on TV,
he wobbled and almost fell.
Maybe the gasp held him up,
righted the wheel of his unicycle,
gave his legs a surge
that powered him across.
As the crowd hauled him off
and carried him aloft,
he thought of the wobble,
how it had tried to send him
down onto the steer-bones
at the ravine's bottom,
his cry echoing out over
the cries of the thousand,
till it suddenly cut off –
and he asked those carrying him
to return him to the ravine,
to his rope, still strung there,
and he took the unicycle,
turned the pedals and sent it
back where it had come from,
alone this time, the crowd quiet,
until halfway across, it fell
with a clatter and a cloud of dust.

CHINESE OPERA

for Charles Simic

She lit the sky with her own fireworks show
at 4am. Up there on her roofgarden,
in her moon & stars dressing-gown
she drained the last of the champagne
then struck the first match. Downstairs,
in the living room, Chinese opera was playing –
the last gift he'd given her with a grin.
She'd played that tape non-stop since then.

He'd laughed until she'd started joining in
with thin quivery vowels stretched and bent,
sobs and cymbal-bashes, and dialogue
spoken in English – her own translations
which varied every time but always
had broken or sacrificed men – and laments
sung in her improvised Chinese, like now
on the roof as she sent the rockets high.

A BLUR

She was a blur when he first saw her.
He was the last into the tent,
his head full of lion growls and the tart
comments of his bank manager.

He stood at the back, scanning the crowd
for his two kids, but his eyes were swiped
by her swinging above him,
over and back and upside down.

She let go and a blond man caught her.
If she'd missed there was no safety net.
He sent his applause round after her
as she bowed in a ring, then ran.

When his kids wouldn't go again
he went alone. He sat in the front
so he could be underneath her
as she turned upside down.

That night, he knew he caught her eye
as she swung above him,
but she was moving so quickly,
if she smiled it was a blur.

The minute she left he left.
He ran around the tent
to catch her going into a caravan,
blue-painted, big enough for two.

He stood outside in the shadows
as she took off her gear
but he took off his glasses,
he wanted to keep her a blur.

OUR IKKY

He's up in the air again,
our Ikky, but he won't get far –
no crow's black wings
are as ramshackle as his,
though they're the third of the year
and the best yet. Bald hens,
broken window-frames,
nails, and string, and glue,
leather, sawn plastic bottles,
green crocodile balloons –
all these helped Ikky's wings
get Ikky up in the air.
But he's not going to stay there.
Last time he got ten yards,
as far as the allotments.
He crashed into a weed fire
and saw turnips. The first time
he never got off the ground.
Look at him now, a giant insect
from Mars, legs dangling,
blue swimming goggles on.
'Ikky, watch out for that plane!'
'Ikky, have you got
your parachute on? Will I
call the hospital?' No sound
from Ikky, as he rises
over the pit museum
and heads for the North Sea.
Will he do it this time, Ikky?
Will he make Helsinki?
I wish him gull-staying-power,
I wish him no sun but wind.

THE MULES

One of them was lame when they bought him
but a rest and a bandage saw to that,
then a week of parsnips and sugar
had him whinnying for the valley,
up which his comrades would canter
at least once daily, carrying panniers
of lemons and olives, newspapers, bread,
goats' milk for the allergic, medicines,
incense, wine for the doctors,
and once a consignment of used Amstrads
that the mules would never forget.
They didn't mind the twisting narrow lanes
that rose from the valley. Even when snow
kept the postman at sea-level,
they slithered down to the village,
and all three of them got used to the hands
of the gentler patients, stroking them
as they stood there chomping daffodils,
or peeing on flagstones, or sleeping
standing up, oblivious to problems
with striking nurses, ward revolts,
doctor burn-outs, or the RAF manoeuvres
that exploded the sky above them.
There were worse outposts for a mule.

INITIATION

Out in the hills, the goat had been easy.
He'd creep up from behind, catch one horn
and enter her. She loved it, he knew,
so he thought he'd start pleasing women.

He stayed in the loo the whole way to London
and found a bedsit in Chelsea. Signed on,
took to hanging out in bars, chatted up
any woman he saw but bedded no one.

He went to museums that were free,
as he'd heard they were good for pick-ups.
He'd heard wrong. Still, the odd statue
had great breasts and he fondled them.

He became a reviewer of strip-shows.
He walked by the canal in the evenings,
keeping a lookout for sex in boats.
He bought a headband and a statue of Cupid.

He knew that soon he'd be overrun.
Meanwhile, he masturbated to a picture
of a woman masturbating, holding a mirror.
At least, this way he wouldn't need blood tests.

At last, he was picked up in his local
by a tall woman and a short one.
They took him home to their basement flat,
took turns with him and with each other.

It was different from the goat, he thought,
as the short woman coaxed him stiff
while the tall one tickled her with a feather.
Ah, the goat, he thought as he came in her mouth.

READING

Yes, I was reading on the M1.
Yes, I was driving, and reading, too –
a book of poems by Paul Durcan,
The Berlin Wall Café, left by my wife
when she walked out. It wasn't
a twisty clifftop road I was reading on,
it was a motorway, and anybody
with one good eye in their head
could drive on that. Didn't I,
as a hitchhiking student, get asked
to drive a car for thirty miles
while the driver slept in the back?
I can't drive, I remember saying.
It's a motorway, he said. Just keep
in the slow lane, and bring her in
at the second next services.
And it wasn't a novel I was reading –
the thing about poems, your Honour,
is they're mostly short. You can look up
between them, or between stanzas,
and see what's happening ahead.
Would you prefer if I'd been swigging
from a hip-flask, or sucking on a joint,
or canoodling . . . ? Never mind that.
And what about that blind driver
whose dog barked at red lights?
I refute the charge of swaying
from lane to lane. I stayed in
the slow lane, did a steady 65.
It was 3am, your Honour, the motorway
was as quiet as it ever gets,
I had no one to hurry home to,
so I took out my Durcan and opened it.
It didn't seem a wrong thing at all.

DONKEY HOOF

A donkey hoof makes the best brooch.
It also makes an excellent soup
and left in the sun, then crumbled,
it is the only true aphrodisiac.
Two donkey hooves mean luck at poker
but three mean a month in hospital,
and anything over three means death.

Ancient Egypt rubbed crushed hoof
into bald heads. I have no record
of its success, but I'm sure it worked.
All a Celtic cowherd needed
was a donkey hoof and a donkey poem
and a young donkey was there to jump on.
A donkey hoof is the best currency.

Hollowed out, a hoof will float –
give one to your favourite toddler.
The lightest donkeys walk on water.
The world is crammed in a donkey hoof.
Petition NASA to blast one up
and loose it among the space debris.

THE BLUE TAPS

He left me the blue taps
from his blue bath.
He left me the cacti he spoke to.
I had to go and take them
from his grey house
before she sold it.
I had to stand there
in the blue living room
and ask her the names
he'd given all the cacti.
I had to leave her
with no taps in the bathroom.
She didn't seem to care.
I wanted to ask her
why he'd been blue-crazy,
or was she in it, too?
I wanted to know
how long they'd taken
to gather fifteen cacti,
and why he'd spoken to them.
I asked none of this,
just ferried my heirlooms
to the back seat of my car.
I hoped the taps fitted.
I hoped I could remember
the cacti's names
in the correct order.
I had a white bath,
but my living room was green.

FRIDAY BED

That casket your mother chose
in Atlanta, Georgia –
black walnut with red velvet,
kept in a back room
for her to lie in
every Friday for two hours,
so she could get the feel of it,
get used to that thin bed,
practise stillness,
       till you
would help her out –
was that the casket
you were nailed into
on her directive, or does she
lie there every Friday still,
or all week long now,
the top half of a bunk bed
with you tucked in below?

THE COMPROMISE

He wanted to be buried on the moon.
At last he was answering the question
but she wouldn't have it. She laughed
and he laughed, but he persisted.
He brought it up at dinner parties.
He wrapped it in a joke, but she
knew he meant it. A guest said
there wouldn't be many at the funeral.
No maggots, though, another said,
and no graffiti on the gravestone,
at least for a decade or three.
She brought up the cost. He shrugged,
spoke of sponsorship, of ice-
preservation, of the enabling future.
He would be famous dead. A guest
proposed a grave on Iona, among
the graves of kings. Mentioned
that only twice had men landed
on the moon, and they were living.
Suggested writing to one. And asking
about grave-sites, she added.
He was undeflected. He repeated
he wanted to be buried on the moon,
whatever it took. He went quiet.
A fifth cork was popped, then he
offered a compromise, a heart-coffin
snug in the hold of a space-shuttle,
his heart in there, the rest of him
in Highgate, in Derry, in the sea.
They were all delighted to agree.

GOODBYE TO THE SKY

i.m. Michelle

Let me tell you a story you'd have liked –
a small plane gets in trouble,
has to come down on a Devon road
and when it bumps to a halt
one wing is over a hedge, the other
sticks skewways into the path of cars,
and the young pilot walks away.
But he wouldn't have known he would,
when the instruments were saying
goodbye to the sky. I hear him
shouting to his wife, his children,
praying for the first time in years,
cursing, even, calling the plane
all kinds of jerry-built junk,
wishing he hadn't been bought
Airfix planes and Biggles books,
remembering his first tonguey kiss
and the last, that morning,
his lovely wife half-asleep
but turning to him, as if continuing
a dream he was happy to share,
unlike this daylit nightmare,
the terrible ground coming closer,
the road a parody of a runway
sandwiched between hedges,
and finally the jolt of the landing,
the best and the worst he'll ever do.
He walked away, that young man,
but you didn't, and your falling
lasted years. Hear this, though –
sticking into that same Devon sky

is a black obelisk, built to remember
the Waterloo dead, its inscription
Peace to the souls of the heroes
and hear it updated, in the singular.

DANCER

Dancing round the pond, she attracted
an audience of men, half-drunk, mainly,
spilling out of the pub to shout
'Take them off, luvvy, what little you've left'
or 'Give us a feel, gorgeous, go on'
or 'If you jump in I'll jump in and save you'.
She paid no more attention to any of them
than she did to the moon or its reflection
or all the miles of black air in between.
Someone began humming a homemade song
that fitted her dancing. Another danced after her,
out of step, unsteady, liable to fall in.
Cars slowed down and stopped, horns blew,
drivers whistled, but she carried on dancing
round and round, steady as a swimmer,
neither fast nor slow, head erect,
and none of the men blocked her path
or dared to approach, and touch her,
not even when, at last, she wheeled away
and danced out of sight, down the hill.

PINCUSHION

A needle in the top of the head?
More in your hands and feet,
all left there for ten minutes —
and you like this? Pincushion,
that's what I'll call you now,
or maybe Porcupine in Reverse,
or Boar Shot in Robin Hood's Forest,
or General Custer. Pincushion's
short enough to stick, so I'll go
for that. Suits you fine, too —
though your woman wouldn't agree.
The needle in your hand driven in
as deep as it would go? You say
it's helping, that you leave there
floating, that home's fine then?
Why do you need to go back, then,
for more needles? Tell me, Pincushion,
do the needles remind you of times
you wanted to be Custer, the day
he got famous? Do you see
Robin Hood in a green dress
in an indoor forest? Isn't there
a boar on your family crest?
Wasn't that needle in your hand
a bit close to the bone? Pincushion,
think about changing to Porcupine.

RUSSIAN

for Steve Regan

He woke up speaking Russian.
He lay there, amazed,
as sentence after sentence emerged
and sailed to the window –
it was verse, it had to be
to flow that rhythmically,
but he hadn't written it,
nor had he been to Russia.

His wife came in from church
to find pages of Cyrillic
on the bed, and her man
on the telephone, in Russian.
He was arguing, she knew that,
though about what?
When had he been to night class?
Was it him here at all?

She remembered the tapes
and his never-right French,
or that time in Prague
at the tram terminus
grasping for a phrase of Czech.
He had to be seriously sick
or possessed. In the pauses
she heard the answering Russian
faintly, a world away.

THE DOG

He was walking an imaginary dog.
He'd stop and yank an invisible lead,
turning to growl at the creature
that he hadn't got all day, that no dog
needed to pee every five yards,
than any minute now rain would fall
from a sky as blue as his one eye.

He brought the dog into the pub.
He tied it to the leg of a chair,
got a pint of stout and sat there
as I followed him in, pretending
to look for someone, then sitting down
with a beer of my own, to stare at him
talking to the dog and to himself.

He drained his glass and got another.
He leaned down and stroked the dog,
muttering to it things I couldn't hear,
straightening up to smile to himself,
then I had to go, out into the November
sunlight, looking behind me, listening
for the faintest whimper or bark.

CROSSING

He rode his horse into the sea and kept heeling it on.
The horse wasn't used to this, but proceeded to swim –
not easy, with the man and those wet jeans on its back –
but it made headway, out into the currents of the Channel
among the yachts, the windsurfers, the long-distance swimmers.
When the Caen to Portsmouth ferry passed, the Captain hooted.
The horse ignored this; the man took off his cap and waved.
Applause broke out among those few passengers on deck.
The man bowed his head into the sea and downed a mouthful.
He spat this out, then spoke for the first time to the horse
whose hooves kept flailing the water, swatting a few lobsters,
alarming squid, missing a frogman by centimetres.
The horse's head was higher now. Had it seen the Isle of Wight?
The man leant down and whispered promises in its ear –
once they hit land, a big bag of oats, a bigger bowl of cider.
He told it that no other horse had made this crossing,
and that once was enough – they'd take the ferry home.
The horse neighed as they passed a rock where a lighthouse
had just switched on, as if they both were expected,
and flashbulbs were ready on the beach, a studfarm waiting.

POSTCARDS

Sailed to Normandy in an afternoon haze,
peered out the window and drank some wine,
saw a dead gull floating on the Channel
and a piece of wood from a broken boat.
Thought of the postcards I could make of those,
how a market was there for cards of the dead –
planecrashes in Andean forests, hidden by leaves;
space-debris; the skeleton of a horse;
a wrecked tank in a Sarajevan suburb;
a pile of clothes left on an empty beach –
nothing as crude as a mutilated body.
I'd keep all my cards black and white
and limit them to a numbered hundred.
Yes, I could see them covering the wall
of the sitting-room I'd hacked out of a cave
on the de-inhabited island I'd bought
with the proceeds of their sale. Around me
ruined crofts, rabbits zapped by myxomatosis,
a lighthouse that last shone in the 20s,
and the north wind blowing me to bone.

AN END

I want to end up on Inishtrahull,
in the small graveyard there
on the high side of the island,
carried there on a helicopter sling
with twenty speedboats following.
And I want my favourite Thai chef
flown there, a day before,
and brought to the local fishermen
so he can serve a chilli feast
before we head off up the hill.
A bar, too, it goes without saying,
free to all, the beer icy,
the whiskey Irish, and loud
through speakers high on poles
the gruff voice of Tom Waits
causing the gulls to congregate.
Get Tom himself there if you can.
And in the box with me I want
a hipflask filled with Black Bush,
a pen and a blank notebook,
all the vitamins in one bottle,
my addressbook and ten pound coins.
Also, a Mandarin primer.
I want no flowers, only cacti
and my headstone must be glass.

ELM

Under the elm tree she died.
No one knew she'd gone there
that March afternoon, after
the botched paella, the white Rioja,
the cycle ride and the swim.
We were bunched around the hammock
taking turns to swing, when Juan
noticed her missing and panicked.
We were used to that, we'd each
known him to ring us at all hours,
asking for her. She was a bee
that garnered her honey elsewhere,
not just at home. She slipped away
while the Scottish diva was singing
a German lament. She wore red,
I remember, a knee-length dress
that brought out her black hair.
She'd over-rouged her cheeks.
When the call came I took it –
I didn't look at Juan, just walked
to the car and drove to town,
like lava was following me.
I braked in the square, by the baker's,
and joined the crowd round the tree.
I saw the cut rope hanging there.
I waited, then pushed on through.

THE BUTCHER

Most nights he climbs from the grave
and makes the trek to the village.
Rain washes the soil off, while the flesh
reconstitutes in the streetlight.
By the old dancehall he has clothes again
including the apron and a bloody cap.
He spits as he passes the supermarket
with its deep-freezes and cellophane.
He stares ahead as he passes the church,
then disappears into the betting shop.

It's then that the noise of the market-place
shuts out the noise of the track.
The ribbons of prize animals he'd bought,
the great hooks that held the joints,
the spike for the customers' accounts –
all these materialise around him
as he sets to sharpening the cleavers
and making the faggots and black pudding.
Already they are leaving the graveyard
and heading his way. They have until dawn.

A PICNIC ON ICE

Let's go back to Mullett Lake in March
and have a picnic on the ice.
Let's wrap up like Inuits, and meet
three miles north of Indian River,
where the jetty stands in summer
front of 577 Grandview Beach.
We'll cram in Lynch's vintage hearse
and motor slowly out onto the ice,
where I'll spread my blue tablecloth
and as it darkens I'll line up bottles –
wine, Zubrovka, poteen if I can get it –
and onion bhajees, chilli beans, tortilla,
goats' cheese and five kinds of bread.
I'll bring a tape of Irish music
to charm the ghosts beneath the ice.
Some of you may act like Michiganders
and cut holes to fish through,
or slip through and swim underwater
like the mad Finns of Minnesota –
or maybe just make needle-holes of piss.
And we might just find time for stories,
the one about the team of horses
that fell through the ice in March –
the current changed, a seam opened,
the ice quaked, a foot became an inch –
and they're down there, skeletons in harness
to a sleigh of logs, past the sunken island's
northern shore, seen a couple times
by the seaplane pilot who told me
over steaks in the Hack-ma-Tack –
and if the ice should suddenly crack
we'll be tipsy, replete, comforted
to be sinking all together with a hearse
down to join the horse-bones on the bottom.

SKYLIGHT

When I stand under it
I feel like a fish in winter
looking up through ice.

This defector from a greenhouse,
this window that wandered,
wanting to be neither horizontal nor vertical,
is my favourite. Bay windows,
french windows, portholes – you can keep them.
I don't want to see mountains.
I like *paintings* of waves.

Only the clouds excite me
with their ceaseless messages –
I learned first of the Gulf War
when I read a cloud.
I successfully warned a chef friend
to avoid a consignment of king prawns
that poisoned a rival's clientele.

Sometimes I photograph clouds through glass.

I heard a knocking once, hard,
as on a door, but when I got up there
the visitor was gone.

SKATING

You'll never be seen skating
on a frozen lake, arms folded,
wearing your hat and long coat,
a tight smile on your lips
as you look into the distance.
You won't even be standing,
looking on, pointing the camera,
the dog gurning beside you
behind his smoky breath,
and the laughter of children
who repeatedly fall, then get up
to skate on again, till night
hides the sky that's crammed
with the next snow. No, you
won't notice the night, stuck
as you'll be, in your blue room,
reading, listening to Coltrane
or Parker, getting up to grab
an oatcake or refill your glass
while outside the snow rises
imperceptibly, till it reaches
the roofs of the smaller houses,
and men and women in dressing-gowns
are skiing between chimneys,
creating a fluid geometry
under the blank-faced moon.

KEEP HIM IN

Keep him back, don't let him out.
Lock the door, keep him in overnight,
make him cover the greenboard
in writing so small he'll need
a magnifying-glass or a telescope
to help him read it back to us.
Leave him different coloured chalks.

Advise him to write in stanzas.
Switch the heating off, but grant him
a half-filled electric kettle,
coffee, and maybe a sandwich.
Call him hourly, to check progress.
(Have a blues playing in the background.)
Tell him he's good, shudderingly good.

Tell him, on the 5th or 6th call,
there's whiskey in the bottom drawer,
but warn him you can't write drunk.
He'll know that, he's turned 40.
Don't hassle him, don't ask what
his lines are about. You'll know
when he reads them out in the A.M.

And you'll have the tape switched on
while you whack him on the back.
His best work, no doubt about it!
Already you glimpse the Russian version.
You know a woodcut for the cover.
Let him out now, call him a cab.
It wouldn't do to overwork him.

THE BAT

In through the open French window
flew the bat, past my head
as I stood peeing into the river
that flowed beneath the house
which the bat quickly explored, round
the barn-sized living-room,
up the cracked stairs, two flights
to the attic where the kids slept
but they wouldn't tonight, not while
the bat stayed. So we opened
the skylight, despite the wasp's nest
on the drainpipe, and I stood
with a glass of the local red wine,
calling to the bat, like Dracula,
Lovely creature of the night,
come to me, I am your friend,
while it looped the length of the room,
with the kids on the stairs, laughing,
but not coming in. And it stayed
past midnight, till Joan
cupped it in her hands
and carried it downstairs
to the same French window,
where I stood, calling after it,
Lovely creature of the night,
come back, I miss you,
come to me, I am your friend.